A Golf Handbook

All I Ever Learned
I Forgot by the Third Fairway

by Jeff MacNelly

Triumph Books

CHICAGO

This book is available in quantity at special discounts
for your group or organization. For more information, contact:

Triumph Books
644 South Clark Street
Chicago, Illinois 60605
(312) 939-3330   Fax (312) 663-3557

Book design by Mike Mulligan.
Typesetting by Graffolio.
Cover design by Salvatore Concialdi.

ISBN 1-57243-115-6

Contents

Foreword

by Dave Barry

I myself am not what you would call an avid golfer. I play golf about once every eight or ten years, when one of my golfing friends talks me into it. I always stress to them that I am not highly skilled.

"I suck," are my exact words.

They never believe me.

"Come on!" they say. "It'll be fun!"

And I have to admit that in some ways it *is* fun. In fact, once I finally get out there on the links (whatever "links" are), I enjoy every aspect of the game of golf, except for the part where you have to hit the ball. And I *really* hate the part when you're at the first tee and you have to hit the ball in front of other guys who are waiting semi-impatiently for their turn.

Naturally all of these guys can hit the ball. I don't know how; the ball, in golf, is ridiculously small and far away. I never, ever, hit it the first time I try. I haul off and swing, but afterward, the ball is almost always still there, sometimes snickering audibly. This is when the other guys start giving me Helpful Hints.

"Keep your head down!" they say. "Keep your left arm straight!"

"MY LEFT ARM IS NOT THE PROBLEM! THE PROBLEM IS THAT THE GOD-DAM BALL IS THE SIZE OF A SUBATOMIC PARTICLE!" This is what I want to shout back at them, although I do not. I just pretend to be grateful for these Helpful Hints, and I keep swinging until the ball is gone. I usually have no idea where it went, and I don't care. I'm just glad it's not in front of me anymore.

I follow pretty much the same process once I get out on the golf course: swing and miss; swing and miss; swing and lose the ball entirely. Sometimes it disappears so completely that I suspect it has gone into some kind of Time Warp, so that it pops out of thin air tens of thousands of years in the past, where it becomes an object of worship for some prehistoric tribe.

So I spend the vast majority of my golfing time driving around on the cart—driving the cart is one of my favorite things about golf—looking for my ball. Often I get separated from whoever I'm playing with, which is good, because then I can actively cheat. I don't mean "cheat" in the sense of "putting down a lower number of strokes than I actually took." I mean "driving to the next hole without even trying to make any strokes at all." In my ideal round of golf, I would just hop in the cart and drive directly to the part of the golf course where they sell beer.

Of course, not everybody golfs this way. Some people—I have seen them on TV—can actually hit the ball almost every time they try, and sometimes can even make it go in the general direction of the hole. You're probably one of these people, which is why you're reading this golf handbook, in hopes of perfecting your game. Let me just say that, handbook-wise, you could not have made a better choice. I know Jeff MacNelly very well, and he is better qualified to produce a golf handbook than any other person I can think of offhand who is a non-golfing professional cartoonist.

So you're in good hands. Study this book; let its wisdom help you as it has helped so many others. Jack Nicklaus, Arnold Palmer, Gary Player, Lee Trevino, and Ben Hogan are just a few of the names of golfers who, tragically for them, were unable to enjoy the benefits of this book. Don't let the same thing happen to you. Let Jeff MacNelly turn you into a better golfer, or at least a different one. And then get out there on the links and show what you can do.

Jeff and I will be waiting in the bar.

Introduction

Golf is a very weird game. It's an addiction to some, an amusement to many, and it's infuriating, at times, to all. But like some crazy old aunt who lives in the downstairs guestroom, we put up with golf because, on her good days, the old girl can be a real hoot.

I'm a social golfer myself. I treat it like my bourbon. I enjoy it immensely in small reverential doses taken with friends. But I treat it with respect, if not suspicion, and I know when to say no. I never drive while golfing, and on those occasions when I feel I must drink and enjoy a round of golf, I use designated golfers and watch it all on television in the safety of my living room.

Driving while Golfing

WRONG

FODE

RIGHT

About the Author

I've never been very good at following directions, so I didn't include very many in this book. I take a relaxed view of the game, which explains why I'm lousy at it, but it's easier to have fun with it this way. Over the years, I've done a lot of *Shoe* comic strips about golf. This leads people to think I must know a lot about it, and that, like all other successful cartoonists, I spend most of my daylight hours on the golf course. The fact is, I draw golf better than I play it.

CHAPTER 1

A Short History of Golf

Viking Origins

The history of golf is as foggy as the Scotland moors on which supposedly it was first played. Scotland to this day has a lot of open pastureland punctuated with various natural hazards such as rocks, bogs, and the odd sheep. And the Scots have a traditional dress code involving lots of plaids, which goes some way toward explaining modern golf attire.

Little is known about who brought the game to Scotland. One school of thought blames the Vikings, a loud bunch of hard-drinking white guys with a penchant for mergers and acquisitions and, of course, yachting. The Vikings would cruise over to visit the Isle of Barra in the Western Hebrides. When they arrived, they would plunder a sheep or two, light a few fires, and generally make nuisances of themselves. They were resented, of course, but they gave the early Scottish tourist trade a much needed shot in the arm. These regular Viking raids came to be known later as Spring Break.

Predictably, adult beverages were served, and the Viking menfolk engaged in a rousing game they called "golaf," which is an ancient Nordic swear word. Early reports describe golaf as a primative team sport, like lacrosse without prep school kids. Fearsome teams of players (today called "foursomes") spent entire weekends bashing a sheep skull up and down the beach with clubs (now called "clubs"). If they made it all the way around the island, then they were said to have completed a "round" of golaf.

The British brought rules, bureaucracy, and real estate to the game. "Golaf" was misspelled "golf," courses were laid out, and equipment was standardized. The clans chafed under the British improvements to the game, and sometime in the late seventeenth century a foursome of brave Scots set out from Glasgow for the New World in search of greener fairways, more reasonable greens fees, and Florida.

Golf in the New World

Golf spread quickly in the New World. Starting on the sheep pastures of old New York, immigrant Scottish Highlanders used their herding crooks to make their shots and found this to be a vast improvement over the primitive clubs of the old country.

The game traveled eventually to all corners of the original thirteen colonies, gradually replacing croquet as the lawn game of choice by the upwardly mobile planters of the day, who had recently invented the weekend.

Golf comes to the
New World

The first public golf courses went up in Massachusetts. The British, looking for a new source of revenue to finance the exclusive golf resorts they were building in Scotland, imposed a series of taxes on golf in the colonies. The colonial golfers rebelled and, on the night of April 19, 1759, sneaked aboard a British trading vessel loaded with overpriced English golf equipment and dumped it into the harbor.

The Boston Tee Party

The game went westward with the expanding new nation. The wide open spaces inspired the settlers as they trudged across the prairie. Advances in irrigation and mowing made golf possible in areas where only the Plains Indians and millions of buffalo once roamed. Vast driving rangelands were claimed and fenced off and sod pro shops sprang up throughout the territories.

The Civil War

The Civil War almost killed off golf in America. The South was doomed almost from the start. They were forced to convert their golf club foundries outside Augusta into munitions factories in a desperate attempt to compete with the industrialized North.

This disparity is still evident today. The more pastoral, agricultural South has a lot of golf courses, while the industrial North has more indoor hockey facilities and automatic pin-setting machinery.

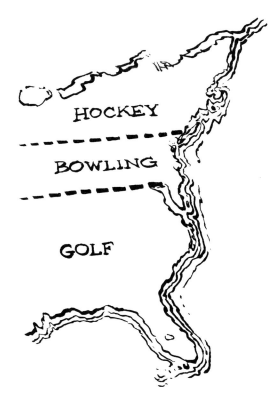

HOCKEY

BOWLING

GOLF

The Civil War
divided
North and South

Modern Times

The game will always be entwined with our history. It became a permanent part of our space program when Alan Shepard hit a golf ball on the moon. It went approximately 2.3 miles on the fly, which is still a record for the longest bunker shot.

CHAPTER 2

Equipment

There is too darn much equipment in your average golf bag. For starters, there are too many clubs. A lousy golfer could play a perfectly respectable round with three clubs: the 2 wood, the 5 iron, and the putter. The great golfers are always sifting through a dozen or so clubs, trying to decide if they should use the 9, the wedge, or maybe a soft 8. The lousy golfer selects whichever club he's most comfortable with—the 5, let's say—and just tries to make contact.

The Ball

The modern golf ball has come a long way. It's now noticeably rounder, but a whole lot harder to hit.

Ball manufacturers have always tinkered with the materials and methods for producing the perfect ball. Today there are buildings full of scientists and engineers devoting their careers to making the ball go farther and straighter.

Evolution of the Golf Ball

1100 A.D.

1400 A.D.

Despite what they tell us, the golf ball is a fairly simple apparatus. Yes, they have special cores made of space-age teflon-creamcheese alloy wrapped in space-age high-tensile rubber bands with a space-age outer coating of hand-rubbed naugahyde. But it is still just a ball that will go directly into the water if you hit it there.

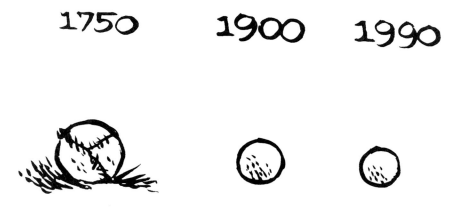

1750   1900   1990

The only thing you need to know about the ball is that it is a sentient being. A lot of people forget this. The ball can hear you, it understands what you're saying, and a good ball knows how badly you golf. So remember to talk to your ball, explain to it where it is you'd like the ball to go, and don't bully it. A good golf ball knows where to go. Your job is to give it some space and let it do its job.

The Tee

This little wooden or plastic device jacks up the ball an inch or so off the turf at the beginning of each hole. It's a British invention that is basically a sanctioned form of cheating. The tee was the first technological breakthrough in the endless quest for a better drive, arriving on the golf scene before computers, wind tunnels, and advertising.

Some say that a good drive should snap the tee in half, but I suspect that's just one more thing to worry about. I like to see how many holes I can play with the same tee without breaking it. Tees are also good to chew on during a round, especially if you're golfing with some health nut who objects to cigars.

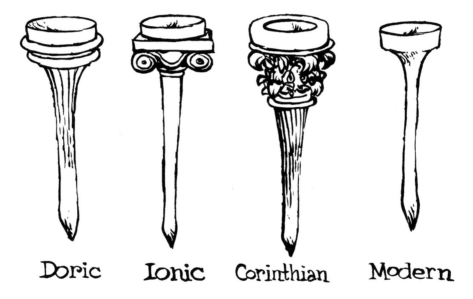

Evolution of the Tee

Doric   Ionic   Corinthian   Modern

The Woods

As we discussed earlier, the first clubs were, well, clubs. Now they are called "woods" because that's where your ball usually ends up after using one. They are basically long sticks with blobs of wood at the business end, except nowadays they make them out of metal. However, since no one wants to have to ask for his "3 aluminum," we still call them woods.

The woods have numbers on them. The longest hitter is the number one, or driver. It's a scary club.

The biggest problem with the driver is that it is the ceremonial mace of the game, only called into service on special occasions when everyone is watching. There's always anxiety attached to the driver which tends to affect its performance. In fact, there have been times when my driver was so nervous I had to bench it for a few holes.

This is where the 2 wood comes in handy. It's a club with a bit more loft than the 1 wood and is used only when there are no more decent shots left in your driver.

The Woods

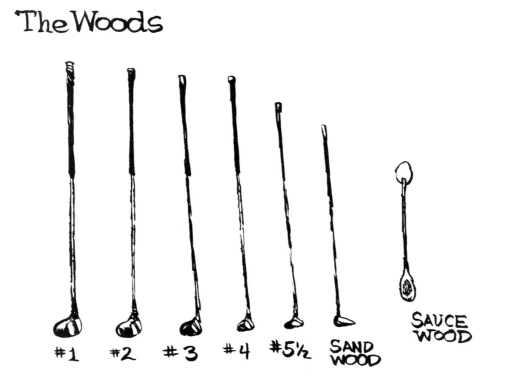

#1 #2 #3 #4 #5½ SAND WOOD SAUCE WOOD

IRONS

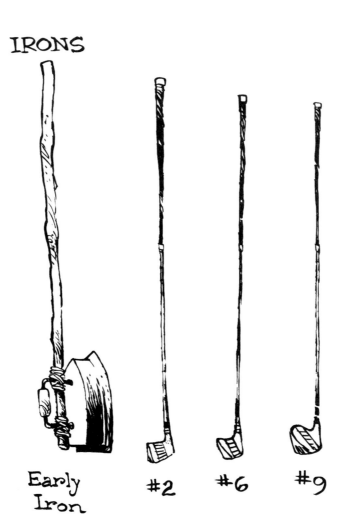

Early
Iron

#2

#6

#9

The Irons

Irons are confusing to the average lousy golfer. There's really not much difference between a beautifully stroked 8 iron and a flubbed 4 iron as far as distance is concerned. So a lot of us just make friends with one iron and use it all the the time.

The Putter

Get to know your putter. Most of your shots are going to be made and missed with this club. Almost as much science has been devoted to putter design as to ball design. They're made of almost any conceivable material and available in many ridiculous shapes. Ignore these and find a comfortable one, one that's pleasant to look at, one that won't cost you too much and that you can trust. Then marry it.

PUTTERS:

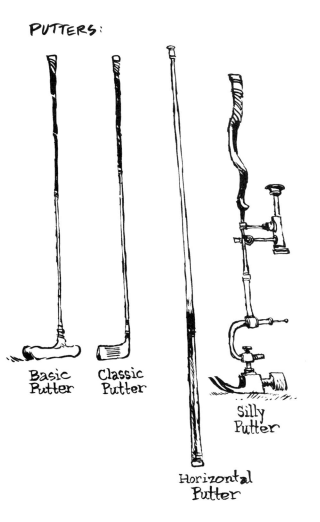

Basic
Putter

Classic
Putter

Horizontal
Putter

Silly
Putter

Bags

The golf bag has evolved from the simple canvas quiver to today's massive chrome and leather contraptions that look like body bags designed by Harley Davidson.

THE FIRST GOLF BAG WAS A SIMPLE QUIVER:

The modern bag has straps for umbrellas, glove compartments, and duffel-sized bins for balls, raingear, first aid kits, and fire extinguishers. And it's getting worse. Now you see these huge traveling cases for golf bags coming down the chutes at baggage carousels, looking like coffins by Samsonite. A family of four going camping for a weekend carries less than most golfers have in their bag.

THE MODERN GOLF BAG

Carts

For many of us, this is the most dependably satisfying aspect of golf. After a lousy shot, we can always escape to the cart, where we are reassured that even though we still can't drive a ball, at least we can drive a golf cart.

Golf cart technology has allowed golf to join boating and snowmobiling as outdoor sports that can be conducted almost entirely on your butt.

The Golf cart of the future

Keep your eye on golf cart research and development. As the cart goes, so goes the game. Already the cart is mandatory on some crowded courses to keep everyone moving at a decent clip. Remember, skiing didn't really take off until someone made it possible for skiers to sit down during the hard uphill part. So look for moveable sidewalks, underground cartways, and robotic caddies.

CHAPTER 3

Golfwear

Project a positive Self-image:

Right

Wrong

Golfwear in general is clothing you would never wear anyplace else. The golf course is the last place on earth where relaxed-fit Sansabelt is not only tolerated but almost required. The game of golf is alone responsible for keeping double knit alive.

Golf has a strange effect on men who ordinarily don't care which tie goes with what shirt and who pad around the house dressed in Giorgio Ourlaundry the rest of the weekend. They go out of their way to get dressed up for a game of golf. They get color coordinated. They wear shoes that look like spats, and they spend a lot of time preening.

If I get a moment to reflect on what I look like, I get those uncontrollable in-church giggles. My mind wanders off to concentrate and I'm left to imagine how I must look playing golf: six feet, five inches, and 240 pounds of slack-jawed determination in funny clothes and borrowed shoes trying to hit a hard white ball that's much too small with a strange stick that's much too long.

Early Scots Hat

Early
20th century

Hats

We'd better start at the top: the golf hat. Many styles have come and gone over the years. The Scottish tam-o'-shanter is a classic, but the fluffy thing on top is a little goofy. I like the Ben Hogan style golf cap, and you still see it around. I think the floppier the better with this model—the look you want is less Payne Stewart and more Henry Fonda in *Grapes of Wrath*.

The baseball hat is the choice of most golfers. Find one with a logo from some famous monster course to get the most psych out of it.

Do yourself a favor and don't wear one of those eyeshade things where your hair sticks out of the top. They make you look like an accountant with a souvenir from the LPGA. What good is a hat without the bag part where your head goes?

Cubs Hat

Headless Hat

The Australian Greg Norman has popularized the cowboy style golf hat. His hat has a shark on it, a bit of a mixed metaphor. These hats make a lot of sense out in the sun, even though they make you look like an outdoor riverboat gambler.

Aussie Hat

Cowboy Hat

The CHI CHI
RODRIGUEZ/
SAM SNEAD
PANAMA

The
Julius
Boros
Pocket
Rocket
Style

Shirts and Pants

Golf shirts are usually made of some kind of slippery knit plastic. The idea is to wear something loose and comfortable that is garish enough for a rescue chopper to spot you in deep rough. Golf pants come in many styles and materials, too, but jeans offer protection from bushes and brambles. I hate snagging an eighty dollar pair of trousers climbing some chainlink fence to retrieve a ball.

It's pretty much up to you what to wear on the golf course, and that's the problem. After all, we're talking about guys dressing themselves here. Historically, getting dressed up has never really been a male strong suit. Women love men in tuxedos because there is practically no chance of selecting an ugly tie with black and white. With golfwear, men are on their own, and, predictably, ugly happens.

The Fat Guy Layered Look

The Summer Fat Guy

However you dress, do everyone a favor and don't wear those sleeveless tank tops. If you are an average guy, chances are your shoulders are fatter and uglier than you think, and we won't even mention the hair part. Save the tank tops for those hot summer days when your plans call for air travel and you're seated next to me. Thanks.

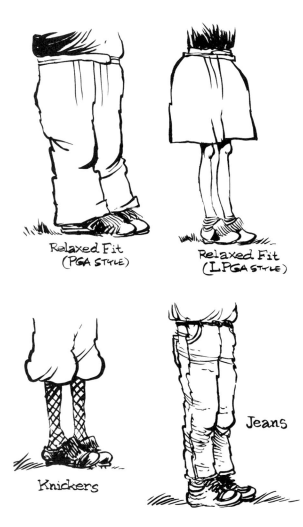

Relaxed Fit
(PGA STYLE)

Relaxed Fit
(LPGA STYLE)

Knickers

Jeans

Shoes

Somewhere between Scotland and the New World, they put a bunch of metal spikes on an old clunky pair of brogans and started selling them as sports equipment. They do a great job of gripping the turf well enough to prevent the rotation of the earth from throwing off your putting, but I use mine mostly to get around after one of our ice storms.

Gölaf Shoes (Viking)

Highland Golf Boot

Early Scots' Golf Shoe

The real reason golf shoes are popular with guys is that they make a distinctive clacking sound on the pavement, the same sound that football cleats made on the way out of the locker room in high school. That's reason enough to wear them, but a good pair of hiking boots with plenty of support is just what you need in a golf shoe for stomping around in the wilderness.

The Modern Shoe

Jungle Boot

CHAPTER 4

The Swing

We've all heard entirely too many theories about the perfect swing, or rather, why your swing is so pathetic. There are a million theories, and the bad news for us lousy golfers is that all of them are basically correct.

The Swing

Getting a Grip

The swing starts with a good grip, and the golf folks have come up with a real twisted one. I speak here of the classic, widely used overlapping grip. This involves placing your right pinky over your left index finger. (If you are left-handed, read this chapter upside down.) This is a reasonable method for grabbing a golf club, and it gets an otherwise useless digit out of the way of your swing.

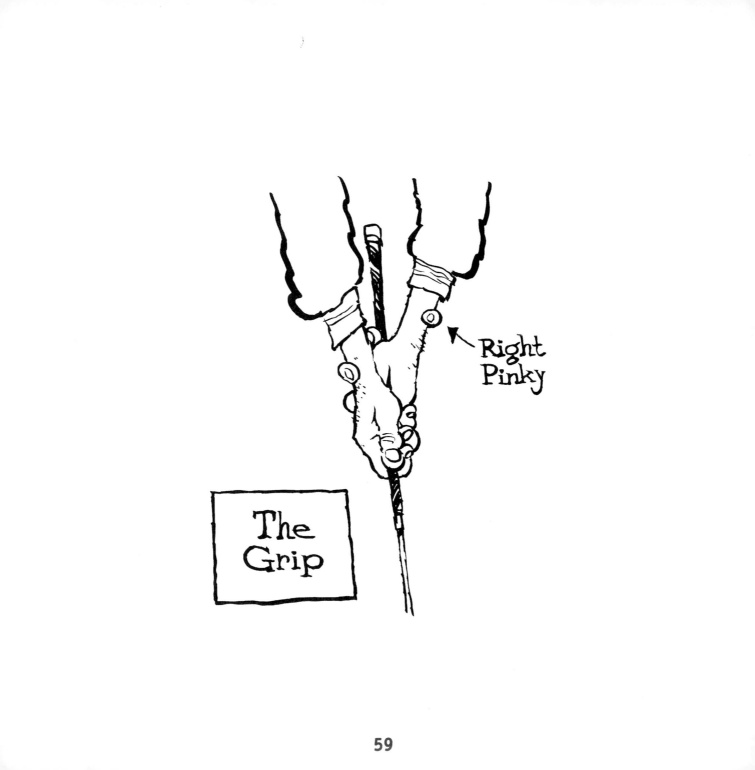

Right Pinky

The Grip

The Basic Swing

Here are just a few things you want to think about while you're attempting a smooth, natural swing:

- Grip the club firmly but not tightly.
- Those little V's formed at the crotch of the thumb and forefinger of each hand should be aligned and pointing at the same place— a spot one inch to the right of your right eye socket.
- Keep your left elbow straight.
- Point your right thumb at the tee.
- Hold your hands high.
- Keep your feet shoulder width apart.
- Toes pointed out slightly.
- Keep your head still.
- Hold your hands high.
- But with the club head on the ground, stupid.

- Place the ball slightly to the left of your center line.
- I guess it's a line somewhere near your center.
- Keep your head down.
- Start the club back slowly.
- Commence shoulder rotation.
- Shift weight to the right hip, but rotate the left one sort of too.
- Do something with the left foot while you're waiting.
- Keep your head down again.
- Stick your left shoulder under your chin.
- Pause.
- Start the downswing, leading with the left arm.

- If your right arm gets to the ball first, you are probably left-handed.
- Begin weight transfer from right to left.
- Come down and through the ball smoothly.
- Weight is moved to the right foot.
- Hips rotate as club follows through.
- Finish with hands high.
- Breathe normally.
- Return your seat backs and tray tables to their upright and locked position.

Clearly this is not the list that Arnold Palmer carried around with him while he developed his swing. After trying to digest all the constantly changing theories and details, it's no wonder we lousy golfers end up flailing instead of swinging.

The Perfect Swing

Remember that you started playing golf in the first place for its relaxing properties and apply these to your swing. Many people will offer to dissect your swing and examine each of its thousand or so components for flaws and clues, and this can be helpful. Dissecting a frog can be educational and fascinating, too, as long as you're not the frog.

Dissecting
your swing:
[not always
a great idea.]

Rhythm

Rhythm is essential to golf, and this is especially true with the lousy golfer. I call this the "shitty shitty bang bang" theory of golf. When a lousy golfer is in the groove, he'll blow two shots, then hit two great ones. Actual pars can result if you're in the "shitty shitty bang bang" groove. Several times I've blown a drive, trashed the recovery shot, then blasted a third shot out of the rough, and sunk a 40-foot putt.

In the Zone

All kinds of athletes talk about being "in the groove," and so do golfers, although they tend to say "in the zone," which sounds a little more unconscious. Lousy golfers are usually out of the zone. This gives us an advantage over more competent golfers. They're shocked by a bad shot. We're always expecting one.

And remember, it's called a "swing" for a reason. It's not a "whack," "wallop," or "hammer." So try to keep both feet on the ground.

CHAPTER 5

Putting

The Putt

What makes putting so frustrating is that anyone can do it. If done right, hardly any muscles are involved. On the rest of the course, a shot involves swinging a big stick, making contact with the ball at a precise point, and propelling it through the air for hundreds, or at least tens, of yards. This feat requires speed, power, and grunting, none of which you see in putting.

My uncle, Ken Fox, out in California, wrote the book on the art of putting. Well, okay, he wrote a book on putting called *Putting in the Zone* which articulates the theory I stumbled on—mental attitude is key to successful putting. Uncle Ken emphasizes that you should make friends with your equipment. If you treat the ball like a balky child or capricious pet and say, "Into the hole, dammit!" you are taking an antagonistic attitude. Look at it this way: the ball's job is to go into the hole. Help it, don't fight it.

MAKING FRIENDS
WITH YOUR EQUIPMENT.

This is a philosophy I can get behind. It puts the responsibility squarely where it belongs: on the ball. Unfortunately, no matter how nice you are to your ball, it won't go where you tell it to go unless you hit it straight.

Putting Myths

You should deep-six some myths about putting that have developed over the years.

1) Just another golf shot

A number of golf poohbahs will tell you that putting is just like all the other strokes you take on the course, only shorter, slower, and a lot funnier looking. So you're supposed to do a smaller version of that flail you executed out on the fairway. Forget it. Putting is a completely different game.

Putting Myth #1
It's just another
golf shot

2) The yips

Famous golfers have admitted to coming down with this mysterious tightening of muscles and mind that makes them jab at the ball and miss even short putts. In other, less sedate, sports we call this "choking," but golfers prefer that it sound like some dreadful disease beyond personal control.

Putting Myth #2
The Yips

3) The lag putt

Here's a beauty. The lag putt is where you putt to get close to the hole. The ball did not sign on to get close to the hole, it's there to go into the hole. Every time.

4) The gimme

If you're left with a short putt "inside the leather," some suave knucklehead will tell you not to bother, it's a "gimme." Sounds gracious? Don't be sucked in, especially if you're playing for cash. Putt out everything. The short ones make a neat sound in the bottom of the cup that you'll be close enough to hear.

The "Gimme" might
become the "Take-ee."

5) Selecting the right putter

Listen, if you stroke the ball right, you could use a two-by-four, and the ball will go in the hole. Any kind of putter will do.

The Right Putter

6) The plumb bob

This is where a golfer squats down, holds his putter between his thumb and forefinger, and gives it a one-eyed squint. I hear this is supposed to help you judge the slope of the green. But even if it did—heck, even if you had a tripod and a surveyor telling you the exact slope—just what are you going to do with that information?

Now that you are on friendly terms with your equipment and unburdened of putting mythology, you need to know about dealing with the terrain out on the green. A few more pointers and then you're on your own.

Distance

If you were allowed to use a measuring tape on the green, you would know exactly how long your putt is, say 26 feet 4 inches from the hole. What does that distance mean to you? Do you have a putting stroke in mind that will propel the ball 26 feet 4 inches? I didn't think so.

The Grain

Grass really does tend to grow in a particular direction. If you need an excuse for why you missed the putt, this is as good as any.

Putting against the grain

The Straight-In Putt

One of the most terrifying shots in golf, we examine the straight putt in a vain search for the excuses we will need if we miss this easy one. The returns trickle in from the sidelines. "Aim a little to the left of center," or "Looks like about a two inch break toward the water." When in doubt, aim the ball at the hole.

Lining Up

All the people standing nearby, since they are human, will be more than glad to give you an opinion. Don't ask. Line up your own putt.

CHAPTER 6

Trouble

Let's talk for a minute about trouble because, face it, it's a major part of your game. However, we lousy golfers can turn trouble into triumph if we plan for disaster.

WHERE THE TROUBLE USUALLY STARTS

The Water

An obvious source of trouble is the water hazard. It comes in many styles and colors on the golf course. There's the huge bunch of water, for example, lakes, channels, inlets, and oceans. There are slightly smaller water hazards, like creeks and ponds. Then you have various types of miscellaneous water in the form of puddles, mostly.

As a lousy golfer, you no doubt are aware of the magnetic force that a body of water exerts on a golf ball. This force acts in concert with gravity to suck golf balls down under the water. The secret to mastering the water hazard, then, is to keep your ball as far away as possible from water's magnetic field. Whenever there is an alternate route available, take it.

What gets us into trouble, as usual, is ego. We see a large body of water between the ball and the hole, and the ego screams, "Go for it, big guy! Blast a 3 wood right over it." Just like on television.

Well, forget it. Get out a nice 5 iron and punt. Go around the water. Your partners may think less of you at first, but they'll change their tune when they splash one, take a penalty shot, and have to shoot from a drop zone on the side of a hill, while you are a stroke ahead and on the green.

The Sand Trap

There is no reason for these to exist except to deliberately cause trouble. Water hazards occur more or less naturally around most golf courses, but sand has to be imported.

Avoid sand traps. If you get into one, you have to haul out your untrusty sand wedge, and no one really knows what will happen after that.

You're supposed to hit down and through the ball, the idea being that the ball will be propelled up and out on this big wad of sand. I don't know about you, but I have a hard enough time guiding the ball with a flat, shiny, metal clubface. Steering it with just sand seems hopeless.

Luckily, as a lousy golfer, you stand a good chance that your ball is sitting up on the surface of the sand, because a ball hit by a lousy golfer will almost certainly roll into the trap. Only really good golfers who can hit high and long end up buried in the sand. And since you are a lousy golfer with no pride, you are free to select something like a 7 iron and flick a little wrist shot up and out of the sand.

The Sand Trap

Chipping

I do this a lot around a green. A good golfer 40 yards out takes a pitching wedge and blasts the ball a hundred feet in the air in a high arch, with backspin and everything, so that it hits the green with a thunk and just sits there. It seems to me that if you hit a ball and it doesn't roll much, you've removed any hope of the ball getting into the hole. I take out a 5 or a 6 and try something called a "chip and run." I like to think of it as a low altitude putt.

Chipping

The Tree

If you're an excellent golfer, trees are tall, pretty things that decorate the rough on either side of the fairway. If you're a lousy golfer, trees are a major part of your game. Your second shot almost always involves a tree or two.

In a typical situation, you find yourself with your ball sitting up on a nice tuft of rough with a big tree directly between you and the pin. Here again, you can use your predictably bad game to your advantage. Rather than trying to shoot over or around the tree, aim right for it. The truly lousy golfer will always miss it by a foot or two.

The Fairway

For the lousy golfer, every shot is a mystery and a challenge. Lousy golfers are at home in the rough; that's where our game is played. We're comfortable hitting out of the mud, the high grass, or the parking lot. The real pressure comes when something goes wrong on the tee and your drive ends up down the middle of the fairway.

We know that the chances of hitting two great shots in a row are steep. When a tee shot ends up in the middle of the fairway by some quirk of fate, the choke factor goes way up, and the excuse factor goes way down. So I think it's only fair to consider the fairway a hazard.

CHAPTER 7

Rules and Etiquette

The reason we have golf etiquette is to avoid fist fights about golf rules. You should probably know a little about each.

The Rules

The original rules of golf, translated from ancient Gaelic, were simple:
- Don't mess around with the ball.
- Hit it if you can find it.
- No whining.

Etiquette

Now that golf is an institution, the rules are a lot more complicated. There are a lot of insane regulations about things like "casual water," "loose impediments," "the influence of an outside agency," "provisional balls," "stipulated rounds," "breach of rule in four-ball Stableford" and so on. If you feel you need to know more about the rules of golf, call a lawyer.

Out on the course, there is one rule that will always get you by: When in doubt, ask your opponent for a ruling. Two wonderful things happen when you ask fellow creatures for their opinion. First, they are flattered and grateful. Second, they give it to you. When you pretend to agree with them, their opinion becomes law. No arguments and, best of all, they owe you one.

Etiquette

If you saw the clowns I usually play with, you would file the term "golf etiquette" under Oxymoron. But I would appreciate it if you would remember a few things.

1) Be quiet when somebody is taking a shot. This is just good manners, of course. I have noticed, however, that we are polite and quiet while some guy lines up a straight three-footer with eight bucks on the outcome, but when some eighteen-year-old kid is shooting a foul shot with no time left in the conference championship game, we're screaming and waving towels in his face.

2) Replace your divot. This is a sound ecological idea for people shooting from a lush lie in the fairway. It doesn't apply to us lousy golfers much. Like skydiving etiquette, it's nice to know, but I don't think I need to write it down.

3) The guy with the ball farthest from the hole is said to be "away" and gets to shoot first.

4) Don't laugh at other people's bad shots. Your game is hilarious enough.

5) On the green, do not step on anyone else's "line." That is, don't put a big footprint in between the hole and anyone else's ball. Unless you can get away with it.

CHAPTER 8

Practice and Lessons

Practice

Practice sounds like a good idea, but don't be fooled. Golf is frustrating enough out on the course without bringing it into your own backyard.

The most diabolical feature of golf is that as one facet of your game improves, another goes in the tank. Practice only accentuates this. Work on your drive, and your short game goes AWOL. Spend a few hours chipping out back, and your putting disintegrates.

Putting is very important, especially in your average lousy golfer's game. On a good day, well over half your shots will be putts. So it might be a good idea to practice putting.

By contrast, practicing your drives is a really bad idea. Your average golf course has three par 3s, so you'll only have fifteen opportunities to use your driver. I, for example, only have seven or eight decent drives in me on a given day. I'm not about to waste them on a bucket of balls.

Lessons

Lessons aren't a bad idea either, but they tend to be too long. Imagine if you could drop by the pro shop and sign up for a five-minute lesson concentrating on the left elbow. That way, your pro gets around to only one or two things for you to work on, instead of delivering a half hour of constant, often humiliating advice.

I had an actual golf lesson once. My teacher was Dave Marr, who went on to win the 1965 PGA Championship.

There we were on the practice tee, this neat compact Texan with a sweet swing and a gawky thirteen-year-old with a sweaty 7 iron. The lesson was not going well. Finally, in desperation, Dave told me to forget about hitting the ball and take a practice swing.

"Relax everything," he said.

I relaxed everything, took a swing, and winged the 7 iron about 200 yards. Those were the last words Dave Marr ever said to me and the best golf advice I ever had.

My only golf lesson

Years ago, I quit golf. It had gotten to the point where my game was totally unpredictable and irritating. Years later, I was lured into a game and an amazing thing happened: lots of my shots went straight. Some were even long and straight. Putts went in. Drives were not embarrassing. I had fun.

I had stumbled onto the secret of improving your golf game: stop playing.

CHAPTER 9

Glossary

ADDRESS THE BALL Before you swing at the ball, talk nice to it.

APPROACH SHOT The shot you think might get you on the green. You usually take two or three of these per hole.

ARNIE Arnold Palmer.

ARNIE'S ARMY The rest of us.

ASSISTANT PRO The guy in the pro shop who has to give most of the golf lessons.

AWAY The guy who is farthest from the hole and who gets the dubious honor of hitting first.

BACK NINE The part of the golf course where your back starts to hurt.

BACK SWING The part of the swing right before the foreswing.

BAG A piece of luggage approximately the size of a Buick designed to accommodate all your golfing equipment, including survival and first-aid gear. Sleeps two.

BALL Hard little round white thing with dimples. Not Mary Lou Retton.

BIRDIE One under par on a hole. Rarely seen. Even more rarely believed.

BITE When a shot with a lot of backspin lands on the green and doesn't roll much. The shot you hit that flies completely over the green also bites, but in a different way.

BOGEY One shot above par. Also a famous actor who was frequently above par himself.

BREAK What a putt does when it encounters a slope on the green. Also, that which you never get in a round of golf.

BUNKER Nice word for "sand trap."

CADDIE Guy who carries your clubs around the course. Also, the car that carries your doctor's clubs to the course.

CART A motorized vehicle that keeps you from walking on the golf course.

CART PATH A path that keeps the cart from driving on the golf course.

CASUAL WATER Water that hangs out on the golf course.

CHIP A short approach shot.

CLUB The instrument that is used to hit the ball.

DIMPLE Little aerodynamic crater on the surface of the golf ball. There are 438 of these on each regulation ball. You can count them.

DIVOT The big hole the golf club makes in the turf after a shot, but somehow also the clod of turf that is removed from the hole.

DOG LEG The big elbow in the fairway that you don't have to worry about since your ball won't go that far anyway.

DOWNHILL LIE When your ball is laying on a downward slope of the golf course. Also refers to the situation when an alibi is unravelling.

DOUBLE BOGEY Twice as bad as a bogey.

DRIVE The shot off the tee, usually taken with a wood. Also what you do in the cart after you tee off, usually toward the woods.

DRIVER The 1 wood.

EAGLE Two under par. A very rare birdie.

FADE A fancy way of saying, "I planned that slice."

FAT A fancy way of saying, "I blew that."

FOLLOWTHROUGH The front end of your backswing.

FOURSOME Four golfers. Grammatical note: You add "some" on the end of a word when you are describing a number of golfers for some reason. Thus, two golfers is a twosome, and an indeterminate number of golfers is a "somesome."

FROGHAIR John Daly's haircut.

FROGSTRANGLER In the South, a strong downpour of rain. Also, this really twisted kid I knew in biology lab.

GALLERY The people who watch golf out on the course.

GIMME The gift—the Trojan horse kind—of a conceded short putt.

GRAIN The direction the little tiny blades of grass on the green grow. Another convenient, and largely invisible, excuse for missing a putt.

HANDICAP A complicated system by which you are awarded charity strokes for being lousy.

HAZARD Any part of the course that causes trouble, i.e., the tee.

HOLE The place where the ball is handsomely paid to go.

HOOK The opposite of a slice, unless you're a lefty.

IRONS The metal clubs. (What about metal woods?)

LADIES TEE Where the guys would rather be teeing off.

LAG PUTT A fancy way of saying your putt is too short.

LIE Where you say your ball is.

MULLIGAN A kind of formalized cheating whereby you get a second chance on the tee shot.

NASSAU A way of losing money in golf.

OPEN A golf tournament closed to all lousy golfers.

PAR The designated average score on a golf hole. The good news about par is that since you are usually over par, that makes you an above average golfer.

PENALTY STROKE A stroke added to your score without your having to take a shot.

PIN The stick with the flag on it that marks the hole. The number on the flag in your pin number.

PUTT The shortest, easiest, and therefore most terrifying shot in golf.

PUTTER One who putts, or that which putts.

RAKE What you use to smooth the sandtrap after messing it up with your footprints and your shot attempts. Also, probably a better way to get your ball out in the first place.

SAND TRAP The place your ball goes to hide when it gets too close to the green.

SAND WEDGE The club specially designed to make your life miserable in the sand trap.

SCORECARD A printed form on which you record your lies.

SHANK Another fancy name for a crummy shot.

SHORT GAME The part of the game that takes place around the green, the short game takes the longest.

SLICE The opposite of a hook, unless you are golfing in the southern hemisphere, in which case the slice goes counterclockwise.

STROKE A disorder where the flow of blood to the brain is interrupted long enough for you to decide to start playing golf.

TEE The elevated, level area from which you start each hole. Also, a small device, usually of wood, which elevates the ball off the turf, in case the tee area isn't elevated enough for you already.

TRAP A big crater in the golf course usually filled with sand, old golf balls, and lousy golfers.

YIPS A nervous disorder you get when you putt too much.